Old WIGTOWN
With BLADNOCH & KIRKINNER
by
Jack Hunter

View from Square, Wigtown

Medieval Wigtown was built on a rectangular pattern, and the building projecting into the street on the right of this picture formed part of the west side of this rectangle. Formerly there would have been another building beyond it, and a corresponding row of houses coming out from Richmond's shop, leaving a small gap or port in the middle. This could be closed at night with a gate, allowing residents to keep their animals secure. Ports such as this, which controlled access to the town, also enabled the authorities to charge visiting traders the dues the town was entitled to levy on them. The first extension of the medieval town was a ribbon development beyond the West Port along the road which split beyond the second car, with one branch going west over the hill to Kirkcowan and the other (to the left) to Bladnoch and the south.

MARKET CROSS   WIGTOWN

© Jack Hunter 1998
First published in the United Kingdom, 1998,
by Stenlake Publishing, Ochiltree Sawmill, The Lade,
Ochiltree, Ayrshire, KA18 2NX
Telephone / Fax: 01290 423114

ISBN 1 84033 025 2

ACKNOWLEDGEMENTS

I am indebted to the following people for providing information:
Mr J. Christison, Wigtown; Mr and Mrs C. Donaldson, Stranraer;
Mr and Mrs G. Gardiner, Wigtown; Mrs C. Vance, Portyerrock;
Mr A. Wallace, Kirkinner. However, any factual errors and all opinions
and conclusions are solely my responsibility.

The smaller and older market cross, surmounted by its pomegranate, originally stood at the east end of the square in front of the town house. When the latter was demolished, the cross was removed for safe keeping and ignominiously lodged in a cell in the town prison. In the late nineteenth century it was liberated, cleaned up, and re-erected beside the new cross. This was erected in 1816, when the town council decided that the burgh required a new market cross, from which 'all proclamations, publications, and intimations shall be made'. Half the cost was met by private subscription.

INTRODUCTION

Wigtown, Bladnoch, and Kirkinner lie close together on either side of the River Bladnoch on the west side of Wigtown Bay. Wigtown, the largest of the three settlements, gets its name from a Germanic language, although there is some dispute as to whether this is Anglo-Saxon or Scandinavian. The Scandinavian 'town or fort on the bay' seems to describe Wigtown's situation very accurately.

It has been claimed that the original town stood a mile to the east on the low ground at the edge of the bay, but this seems unlikely given the natural advantages of Wigtown's present location. The town's position, overlooking both Wigtown Bay and the first crossing over the River Cree, made it a place of strategic and commercial importance. Edward I recognised this in the thirteenth century, declaring the castle to be a royal castle and appointing governors to it. Faint traces of this stronghold are still visible today in the first field on the left on the road to Wigtown harbour. The first written reference to the town occurs at the end of the thirteenth century. In 1341 it was created the chief town of the Earldom or County of Wigtown, and its status as a royal burgh probably dates from this time, although the existing burgh charter is dated 1457, the original apparently having been lost.

Wigtown benefited commercially from its harbour (busy with coastal rather than foreign trade), its fairs and markets, and its jealously guarded right to levy dues on all sheep, cattle, and wool crossing the River Cree. This right was still exercised in the late nineteenth century and was applied to livestock travelling by rail on the Dumfries to Stranraer line. However, the coming of rail transport and the advent of the internal combustion engine relegated Wigtown to the periphery of the communications network, and its trade and prosperity suffered. During the twentieth century it has also ceased to be the area's seat of administration and justice. Wigtown's new position as Scotland's official book town may help to revive something of its former prominence.

The origin of the name Bladnoch has defied all reasonable explanation, although the reason for the village's existence is clear. It stands at the first crossing - originally a ford and later a bridge - of the river it is named after. The main route from Edinburgh and the north has always bypassed Wigtown and headed straight for the river crossing. The old road, much used by pilgrims bound for Whithorn, ran half a mile west of and parallel to the present road by Fordbank and Trammondford to Culquhirk. Traces of it can still be seen on the B733 a few hundred yards west of Trammondford crossroads, where it crossed the road to Kirkcowan. A line of bushes and trees on the hillside to the north of the B733 marks the course of the old road. This particular stretch is known locally as 'mushy mortoun'.

Like Wigtown, which provided accommodation for travellers at the friary, and Bladnoch, with its ford, Kirkinner has important links with the great pilgrim route to Whithorn, Scotland's principal place of pilgrimage in the Middle Ages. Kirkinner grew up round an early chapel serving pilgrims bound for Whithorn. Evidence for the existence of such a site comes from the discovery in the churchyard last century of two tenth century carved stone crosses of the Whithorn school of sculpture. One of those now stands in the parish church nearby (the other has been lost). The church and barony were originally called Carnesmoel, the modern name probably coming into use in the sixteenth century. The village is now called after St Kennera, who was martyred at Cologne in the fifth century.

With an ancient religious site, but no industries, Kirkinner complements Bladnoch, its neighbour of two miles distance. Bladnoch seems never to have had a church but has been the home of various industries of more than merely local importance. This century both villages, together with Wigtown, have looked to Bladnoch Creamery as the area's major employer. All three communities were much affected by the presence in their midst of the wartime airfield at Baldoon, the most recent example of many close ties which have linked the settlements for hundreds of years.

The oldest part of Wigtown was built on a rectangular pattern common in medieval Scottish towns. North and South Main Street, on the right and left, form the long sides of the rectangle, while the two buildings jutting out from North Main Street, just visible above the trees in the centre, mark what remained of the short, west side of the rectangle when this picture was taken. The fourth, east side was formed largely by the town house or tolbooth, the tower of which provided the photographer with his vantage point for this shot. Hens and other livestock once wandered freely in the area in the centre, which was also where Main Street householders kept their middens (refuse heaps). In 1809 it was enclosed by the town council and planted, with the subsequent addition of the bowling green and, later, tennis courts.

North Main Street from the west. The gable two-thirds of the way along the street marks the place where a building was demolished *circa* 1842 to improve access to the town from the north (New Road). The second building beyond the gap is the Old Red Lion, a former coaching inn now demolished and replaced by flats. The premises of Mr McKeand, saddler and ironmonger, are a reminder of Wigtown's traditional role as the service town for the surrounding agricultural area. In the late nineteenth century the building on the near side of the sun awning was the headquarters of Mr Gordon Fraser, a notable entrepreneur, whose books on Wigtown are the most authoritative sources of information on the town's past.

South Main Street, Wigtown.

962/35

South Main Street from the west, with the trees of the square on the left. The Galloway Arms Hotel is still standing, but the building has been converted into private flats. As well as being a hotel it was also a coaching inn, fulfilling the same role in the days of horse transport as a modern railway or bus station. The Richmond family, whose former premises are visible in the previous picture, traded from this shop until the late 1940s. The building nearest the camera was the Clydesdale Bank, one of three banks in Wigtown at the time.

MAIN STREET AND MARKET CROSS. WIGTOWN   86666. JV.

From outside the West Port it is possible to see the end of one of the two original routes into Wigtown from the north. Called the High Vennel, it comes down between the second house on the left and the building beyond which projects into the street (the lady immediately behind the cart is about to cross the High Vennel). The newer of the town's two market crosses dominates the scene. Behind it are the bandstand and combined bowling and tennis pavilion, which occupied the west end of the tree-lined square.

The present County Buildings stand on the site of the original town house or tolbooth, which formed the east side of the medieval street pattern. A small eastward extension of the rectangle (left background) ran down the side of the tolbooth towards the harbour with the East Port at its end. This extension is the modern Bank Street and the East Port probably stood opposite the present Wigtown House Hotel. The bowling green has always been situated in the square. Founded in 1830, the club is one of the oldest in the country.

Wigtown's first tolbooth, in existence in 1591, was demolished in the eighteenth century by the drastic expedient of gunpowder. Its successor was more kindly dealt with when it required replacement: part of it was retained, including the tower, and the present building constructed round about it. Consequently, the window at ground level at the foot of the tower is said to be the cell where the famous Wigtown martyrs were imprisoned prior to their execution in 1685. The existing building was erected in 1862 using sandstone shipped in from north-west England. Its name is a reminder that Wigtown was the county town of Wigtownshire and that the county council for some time had its headquarters there.

The view of Wigtown from Windy Hill is a rather untidy one. The line of houses running to the right behind the small building in the field is the High Vennel, one of the original roads into Wigtown from the north. The continuation of this route is indicated by the dyke running to the left from the building in the field. On the extreme left is the chimney of the town gasworks and to its right one of the town's several former schools, the Bladnoch Charity School.

Something of a mystery here: since the building is the town's former cleansing depot in New Road, the prize-winning horse should be the one which pulled the dust cart. However, such an animal would not normally be used for breeding purposes, as this one clearly has been. Had the town council invested in a dual-purpose animal? No mystery, however, surrounds the cause for celebration: the horse has won first prize, probably for harness and saddlery, at the annual Wigtown Agricultural Show, held since 1811 until today on the first Wednesday in August. It may be that the photograph was taken while the building was still owned by a local farmer.

The cyclist stands at the entrance to Agnew Crescent and the photographer at the foot of High Street. The first shop on the left belonged to a well-known photographer of the late nineteenth century, Alan M. Nicolson, some of whose work appears in this book. An underground stream, the Pultroit, is said to cross the street just where the mounted cyclist is positioned in the middle of the picture.

JV 58412

In this view from the top of High Street looking east the hills on the other side of Wigtown Bay can be glimpsed on the right of the County Buildings. Wigtown's position on the sheltered eastern side of a hill overlooking the bay has been vital to its development. The buildings in the foreground on both sides of the street have long disappeared. Prominent in the centre of the picture are the trees surrounding the square, which were the home of numerous crows. These were the subject of a lengthy, heated town council debate in 1875, when a motion to expel the crows was narrowly defeated and the affair reached the national press.

High Street, Wigtown.

High Street, with the road westwards to Kirkcowan disappearing over the top of the hill. When High Street was first built in the eighteenth century, it was so narrow that two carts could barely pass each other. The congestion was resolved when the street was rebuilt with the houses set further back from the road. The tallest building on the left is the Oriental Hotel. J. Burke's butcher's shop later became a garage and the scene of a suicide.

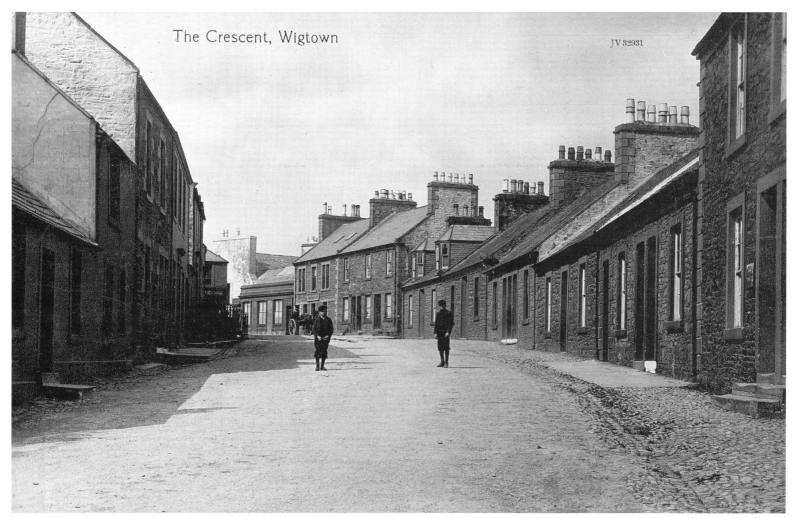

Agnew Crescent looking towards the junction with Main Street. The street gets its name not from the famous family of hereditary sheriffs of Wigtownshire but from the first person to build a house there when the street was laid out. Prior to that time a few houses had already existed on the left-hand side. The second two-storey building on the right was home to Mr W.J. Gunning's butcher's business for much of this century. The building two up from it housed the Wigtown Ex-Servicemen's Club in the 1920s and 1930s.

Acre Place, Wigtown.

This photograph of Acre Place was taken at almost exactly the same spot as the previous picture, but this time looking south down the Bladnoch road. Until the new housing schemes of the 1930s were built, Acre Place stood almost at the edge of town. Kilquhirn Lane branches off immediately beyond the small tree in the right foreground; its name suggests the existence of an early chapel in this area. The stables beyond the houses on the left were the original home of the burgh's dust cart and horse. The dustman, Dan Finnegan, was also the town's lamplighter. In an adjacent building butcher W. Gunning bred chinchilla rabbits.

Acre Place again, but in very different weather conditions. With its proximity to the sea and the North Atlantic Drift, Wigtownshire sees very little severe winter weather, although it does occasionally suffer snowstorms. The most notable ones of the last fifty years occurred in 1941 and 1947, this being a much earlier example. Just at the lamp-post on the left a drive leads down to a villa called 'Orchardton', the home in the late 1940s of a well-known film actor, James Robertson Justice, who appeared in the popular 'Doctor' films. During the 1947 snowstorm he went skiing on a hill outside the town, probably the first time the sport had ever been practised in the district.

When a new harbour was built in a different location in 1817, it was necessary to construct a road to it, and Harbour Road leaves the main square at its south-east corner (above). The building in the middle of the picture is the former parish church manse, built privately by the Rev. Peter Young, who died in office in 1864 at the age of 92, having been parish minister for 66 years. The tall building on the right is the former City of Glasgow, later National, Bank, with the car of an obviously well-to-do customer parked outside. The small building with the prominent chimney next to the bank was the office of Mr M'Lean, a solicitor, who was also county clerk.

A picture taken from well down Harbour Road looking northwards towards the town centre. The building on the left, with its numerous distinctive chimneys, is the former prison for the Machars district of Wigtownshire. Despite its considerable size, the local newspaper reported in 1853 that it was seriously overcrowded, housing 18 prisoners when it had been designed for only 9. By the 1940s it housed prisoners serving short sentences and was closed soon after and converted to a private house. Beyond it and the trees on the left is Southfield Park, the home of the Wigtown Agricultural Show until 1991.

The most famous place in Wigtown, commemorating the most celebrated event in the town's history. According to tradition, two women, 18 year old Margaret Wilson and 63 year old Margaret M'Lauchlane, were executed by drowning at Wigtown in 1685. Their Covenanting and Presbyterian co-religionists claimed they were killed for their adherence to their faith, while the Episcopalian government said they were executed for treason in refusing to acknowledge the king's authority. It was perhaps the worst incident of the Killing Times, the most violent phase of the religious troubles of the seventeenth century, although there is some controversy over whether the executions actually took place. A strong local tradition that they did is countered by a lack of contemporary written evidence and the fact that a reprieve was issued. The fittest verdict is probably the uniquely Scots one of 'not proven': the available evidence does not permit a decision either way. Whatever the truth, these tombstones in the old churchyard mark the traditional graves of the two women.

The wooden stake, now replaced by a granite cairn, marks the traditional site of the martyrdom. Until the Bladnoch changed its course in the early nineteenth century, leaving its former channel to silt up and become salt marsh, this used to be the river bed. An early print reveals that it was also the site of the original Wigtown harbour. The embankment of the Newton Stewart - Whithorn railway, which reached Wigtown in 1875, runs across the middle of the picture. The house on the knoll behind is Croftanrigh and the surrounding field therefore the possible site of Wigtown friary. The cramped nature of this spot has led to speculation that the friary was in fact situated further back up the hill, opposite and just above the parish church (left, background).

Botany Street runs down to join High Vennel at the latter's north end. The name probably derives from the convict settlement at Botany Bay in Australia since this area housed poor and not very welcome immigrants to the town, chiefly from Ireland. The building in the right foreground was the town's lodging house, which catered for the impoverished and needy. Ironically, modern Wigtown's most upmarket private housing estate is situated in the field just behind where the photographer was standing.

JV 32925

The new harbour was built after the Bladnoch changed its course in 1817. Its appearance here at high tide is deceptive, for the huge range in Solway tides between high and low water (20 feet at nearby Kirkcudbright) means that at times the harbour consists mainly of mud banks. But the reason for the port's decline was not the tide; instead, the small house on the left in the middle distance holds the answer. This is the station-master's house (the station is just out of shot to the left). The coming of the railway ended Wigtown's days as a seaport. However, after a major renovation made possible by a government-funded scheme in the 1970s, the harbour is once again in use for pleasure boating, as perhaps foreshadowed by the three young gentlemen in the rowing boat.

Several previous pictures have shown gas street lamps, and this is a fine shot of the town gasworks in North Back Street, now Lochancroft Lane. Built in the early nineteenth century by a private company of local businessmen, the works later passed into the ownership of the town council, closing down after the Second World War. Low Vennel, which complemented High Vennel as the second traditional route into the town from the north, is on the right. New Road, which replaced the vennels as the main thoroughfare into Wigtown, is on the left. The houses running across the picture between the two mark the line of North Back Street, a lane which ran along the bottom of the back gardens of North Main Street houses. A similar lane on the south side of the town was called South Back Street or, locally, 'the Back Sides'. These lanes formed the northern and southern boundaries of the medieval town.

Although Wigtown's grammar school was the oldest in the county, it does not seem to have had its own building until 1712. This had become too small within 70 years, and in 1781 the town council instructed the school-master to hire a room in the town as an overflow classroom. Because of the 'exhausted state' of the burgh's finances, the cost of hiring this room was to be met by charging the 'stranger schollars' more than the 'town and parish schollars'. The modern Wigtown Primary School is still housed in the building shown here, dating from c.1850, albeit shorn of its tower and with major extensions added. When it was first built it was much smaller, consisting of the part to the left of the front door back to the protruding gable. Its two classrooms had a sliding partition which, along with a pulpit, allowed the school to double as a church. This makeshift arrangement prevailed while the old parish church was being demolished to provide the building materials for its successor. The partition and pulpit were still in place in the 1940s.

LIGHTLANDS TERRACE, WIGTOWN.

214664 J.V.

Lightlands Terrace was the first of the new local authority housing to be built. The mock-Tudor villa at the left of this picture was the home and surgery of a prominent citizen, Dr Lilico, the town's doctor in the 1920s and 30s and a well-known breeder of Border terriers. The bus, approaching sedately from Agnew Crescent and *en route* to Whithorn, was owned by the Caledonian Omnibus Company.

Copyright
Wgn.71

From Monument, Wigtown

Raphael Tuck & Sons
Ltd.   London

Corresponding to the housing developments to the west in the 1930s were two schemes on the north side of Wigtown. The white bungalows on New Road are just visible in the middle distance on the left, while the houses of Jubilee Terrace, foreground, were built in 1935, the year of King Edward and Queen Mary's Silver Jubilee. The generous space between the blocks raises eyebrows today. Creetown granite quarries are on the opposite side of the bay, with the granite crusher at their foot on the water's edge. From left to right, gasworks chimney, parish church steeple (the gift of Lord Galloway), and County Buildings tower punctuate Wigtown's skyline.

U.F. CHURCH, WIGTOWN.

RELIABLE ... SERIES ...

Now demolished, this building stood at the edge of Wigtown on the road from Kirkcowan. A town plan of 1832 describes it as the Seceder's Meeting House. It was built in 1750 and while it was under construction the congregation worshipped on the green at the back of the church. Having changed its name several times following union with a number of other churches, it finally ended up as the Wigtown West Church of Scotland in 1929. In 1947 it was sold to Mr Noah Henry, proprietor of a travelling fun fair, for use as a store, and when he disposed of it the building was taken down.

Bladnoch

The essential character of the village of Bladnoch is encapsulated in this picture, which includes four-fifths of the settlement but omits the commercial and industrial quarter, out of sight on the left along with the road bridge and the distillery. The viaduct in the foreground carried the Newton Stewart - Whithorn railway across the river and was one of the most costly constructions on the line. Although the girders have long since been removed, the central pier and abutments are still a prominent part of the local scene. A short distance along the line to the left was the siding that served the Bladnoch Creamery. For almost all of its ten year independent life, Thomas Wheatley held the franchise to run the Wigtownshire Railway. His ability to operate the line efficiently on a shoestring budget by miracles of engineering ingenuity became legendary, and the line was always known locally as 'Wheatley's Railway'. He lived at 'Woodside' at the edge of Wigtown on the Bladnoch road.

BLADNOCH.

A close-up of part of the previous picture, taken from the south-west rather than the south-east. The large house on the left belonged to Mr Lennox, who ran a coal business in the village; the small, white house beside it was a general store owned earlier this century by Mr Charles Ertel; the roofed entry beside Mr Ertel's shop led to Anderson's iron foundry. It may seem curious to suggest that Bladnoch had a commercial and industrial quarter, but at the end of the nineteenth century it boasted, besides an iron foundry, a coach-building business, a distillery, and a joiner's shop, with a potato manufactory and farina mill just outside the village. In 1899 a creamery opened across the river. At the time Bladnoch had three grocers' shops, a large tailoring business belonging to Mr M'Clumpha, a post office, two inns and a bowling green, the latter presented by the Earl of Galloway.

BLADNOCH.

The west end of Bladnoch with the road bridge just out of shot to the right. In the foreground is the Galloway Inn, perhaps the oldest building in the village and known locally as 'the end hoose'. To its left Messrs Nivison and Rennie's coachworks, where carriages of the horse-drawn variety were built and repaired, is just visible. Judging by the size of the houses, Bladnoch seems to have been another of those places where the west end was the home of wealth and power.

Bladnoch distillery, built in 1817 by the brothers Thomas and John McClelland, is situated at the west end of Bladnoch, upriver from the bridge. It remained a family business for almost 100 years, experiencing varying fortunes. These variations continued after it passed out of the McClellands' hands, with periods of closure alternating with times of prosperity. In 1980 production was 350,000 gallons per annum but the final owners, United Distillers, closed the plant down in 1993. However, the distillery has remained open as a visitor centre with conducted tours of the works, and in 1997 the prospect was held out of a resumption of whisky production.

The distillery buildings were grouped round a central yard; this picture shows the rear of the south range with the manager's house on the left. Before the Second World War most of the malt whisky produced went for blending, although a little was marketed under the label Brae Dew. Post-war the output was bottled and marketed as Bladnoch Lowland Malt Whisky, which is still available. Bladnoch was the most southerly distillery in Scotland.

Water from the nearby river was used in the distillery both as an ingredient in the whisky and to drive a water wheel, which originally powered all the machinery. Because the Bladnoch is tidal to just above the bridge, the water for the distillery had to be taken from half a mile further upstream, and brought down by a lade, shown here. The lade or cut gave its name to the narrow strip of land between it and the river, seen in the middle of the picture. Generations of Bladnoch and Wigtown children went 'up the Cut' in summer to swim at Linghoor, the best bathing place on the river - 'far fam'd Linghoor' as the Kirkinner-born writer Samuel Robinson described it. The two-arch Bladnoch bridge was erected *c*.1860 to replace one built 150 years before.

Fordbank, on the back road bypassing Wigtown, looks much the same today, although the industrial buildings out of shot to the right have been demolished. Now a hotel, it was originally home to Mr George McClelland, owner of the adjacent 'Preserved Potatoe Manufactory and Farina Mill'. Farina was potato meal, a poor quality food supplied to those not in a position to complain: Mr McClelland was 'contractor to H.M. Government'. The 'tattie mill's' other product was patent preserved potatoes, a forerunner of instant mashed potato, although at the end of the nineteenth century, port, sherry, burgundy, and champagne were produced there too. Mr McLelland was a member of the family who owned the nearby Bladnoch Distillery, and it is thought that his wine-making exploits were a hobby rather than a major commercial interest.

Of all the industries located in Bladnoch, the creamery was in continuous operation the longest, and was the largest employer in the Wigtown area. Established in 1899 by the Scottish Co-operative Wholesale Society to take advantage of the transport facilities offered by the Wigtownshire Railway (foreground), its closure in the late 1980s was an enormous blow to the district. Soon after opening it expanded beyond the single building in this picture to include a margarine factory producing SCWS's own-brand Bluebell margarine. Although this was the creamery's principal product, of which it was the sole manufacturer, it also made cheese (winning the world championship on one occasion), butter, and cooking fat. Today the buildings house an industrial estate.

In 1669 these ruins, a mile east of the creamery, were the scene of a tragic event commemorated in opera, Sir Walter Scott's *Bride of Lammermoor*, and local folklore. Janet Dunbar of Carsecreugh near Glenluce, daughter of the first Lord Stair, was compelled by her mother to marry David Dunbar of Baldoon and give up the impoverished suitor Lord Rutherfurd whom she wished to wed. Nineteen days after taking up residence at Baldoon she died, unleashing a torrent of sensational rumour and speculation. Several versions of events exist, one describing the disappointed suitor, Lord Rutherfurd, lurking in the grounds before entering the bedroom and attacking the groom, with the unfortunate bride accidentally being killed when she tried to intervene. Even more lurid alternatives involve the bride's insanity or the intervention of the Devil himself. Local people still believe the ghostly White Lady of Baldoon haunts the place of her premature death.

This house replaced the old castle of Baldoon. The farmland surrounding Wigtown is some of the best in Galloway. In the late seventeenth century Sir David Dunbar of Baldoon pioneered modern methods of cattle rearing, keeping a thousand head of cattle in a great park two-and-a-half miles long by one-and-a-half miles wide. About four hundred animals were sent yearly to the English markets.

In the Second World War Baldoon Park became an RAF airfield, where aircrew other than pilots were trained. Many of the airmen were from countries of the then Empire and German-occupied Europe. Careful scrutiny reveals Bladnoch village on the extreme right with the creamery in the line of trees on the near side of the river. The line of the railway can be traced running past the creamery and then left the whole way across the picture. It divides the airfield in two, with the functional part in the foreground and the living quarters and messes some distance away almost in the centre of the photograph, taken in 1942. *Photograph (WI/12/7) reproduced by permission of the Royal Air Force Museum, Hendon.*

The clachan of Braehead lies a mile south of Baldoon: the site of the airfield is just beyond the line of trees in the middle distance on the right. Braehead grew up round a small industrial complex on the banks of the Markhill Burn (the burn crosses the picture from left to right, unseen, in a small valley). Milldriggan Mill house, the white building in the centre, stands on the far side of the burn. As well as the corn mill, there was a joiner's shop and sawmill, a flax mill, and a smithy. The large building nearest the camera, 'Glenarrow', was built *c*.1918 by the then owner of the sawmill and joiner's business, Mr Skimming. The Skimmings, however, did not occupy it and the house was bought by a prominent local farmer, Mr James Christison of Barglass. On the right is the embankment of the Wigtownshire Railway.

The present Milldriggan Mill (no longer in operation) dates from the nineteenth century, although a mill has stood here since the Middle Ages. Like the rest of the Braehead industrial complex, it used the waters of the Markhill Burn, which was straightened and deepened from half-a-mile upstream to provide the necessary flow. The last owners were the McDowalls, a well-known family of millers, who worked Milldriggan for nearly 140 years. In the Second World War one of the family, Sgt Pilot Andy McDowall, DFM and Bar, flying with 602 City of Glasgow squadron, was one of 'the Few' who helped to win the Battle of Britain. In the later stages of the war, as a Wing Commander, he led the RAF's first jet fighter squadron.

GENERAL VIEW, KIRKINNER

Copyright Knr. 8

Kirkinner, barely half a mile south of Braehead, probably owes its existence to an early religious site, conceivably where the present church now stands among the trees to the left. This view from the railway station shows the village hall on the right and the school - rebuilt after the disastrous fire of 1920 - on the left. At the start of the fourteenth century the Kirkinner minister was Alexander Bruce, brother of King Robert. Ironically, he was appointed by Edward I. Although granted the rectorship of Kirkinner or Carnesmoel, as it was then known, Alexander probably never lived there. Andrew Symson, minister in the late seventeenth century, wrote the first comprehensive description of Galloway.

The timetables displayed on the front of the station date this picture to between 1885 and 1923, when the Newton Stewart to Whithorn line had passed into the ownership of the Portpatrick and Wigtownshire Joint Railways, consisting of the four big companies named on the boards. Kirkinner station's heyday, however, came during World War II, when it was the halt for the nearby airfield, RAF Wigtown, with its population of 1,600. The roof of the station-master's house is visible just to the right of the station buildings. These have all now disappeared and the site is occupied by two bungalows.

Kirkinner, with the station-master's stone-built house visible at road level at the end of the street. The railings on the left mark the entrance to the village hall; the Railway Inn is the second building beyond them. In January 1943 an Anson aircraft approaching RAF Wigtown crash-landed on the hill behind the station, fortunately without injury to the crew.

Kirkinner pupils outside the school (out of shot to the left), wearing the same unofficial uniform as their fellows in nearby Wigtown: white pinafores for the girls and celluloid collars for the boys. Although it is obviously not winter the children all have shoes on, unusual at the turn of the century, when almost all country children went barefoot during the summer months.

On 16 April 1920 Kirkinner school and schoolhouse were destroyed by fire. The blaze started in the early evening in rooms above the school which formed part of the school-master's house. It was first noticed by neighbours, who, led by Mr James Potts of the Railway Inn, vainly tried to contain the fire. A strong wind fanned the flames, which were seen for miles around, and the fire gutted the building. The entire contents of the school, including desks, piano, and library, were destroyed, but thanks to the efforts of local people a few of the schoolhouse furnishings were saved. The school-master, Mr Williamson, and his wife and daughter all escaped unhurt, although Mrs Williamson had a narrow escape when the roof of a room collapsed while she was trying to rescue possessions from it. This picture shows the rear of the school with the school-master's quarters at right angles to it.

TORHOUSEMUIR HOUSE.

The mansion house of Torhousemuir or Balmeg estate stands three miles west of Wigtown just north of the Wigtown to Kirkcowan road. The older part of the house (left) is an enlargement of the original thatched dwelling which was built several hundred years ago. The extension at right angles was built in the late 1800s by the McHaffie family, who owned the estate for much of the nineteenth century. They had close connections with Wigtown: one was provost of the burgh while another was son-in-law of John Black, a notable Wigtown solicitor and banker. James McHaffie, a professional soldier, distinguished himself in the 1812 war against America and finished his career as a lieutenant-general.

Corsemalzie House.

Corsemalzie House, seven miles south-west of Wigtown on the B7005, is now a hotel. It is mentioned by the author Gavin Maxwell, who was brought up at neighbouring House of Elrig, in his book of that name. While looking for birds' eggs, the youthful Maxwell and his brother met the owner of Corsemalzie, who shared their enthusiasm and became friendly with them. Maxwell describes Corsemalzie as 'a big grey stone house with an unkempt lawn from which scores of rabbits scuttled into the rhododendron undergrowth'. The wide moorland countryside surrounding Corsemalzie and the lives of its human and animal inhabitants have been memorably described in several books by the writer Ian Niall, who, like Maxwell, spent his childhood in the area.